# 42 Juicing Solutions for the Common Fever:

Reduce and Lower Fevers without Recurring to Pills or Medicine

By

Joe Correa CSN

## COPYRIGHT

© 2018 Live Stronger Faster Inc.

All rights reserved

Reproduction or translation of any part of this work beyond that permitted by section 107 or 108 of the 1976 United States Copyright Act without the permission of the copyright owner is unlawful.

This publication is designed to provide accurate and authoritative information in regard to the subject matter covered. It is sold with the understanding that neither the author nor the publisher is engaged in rendering medical advice. If medical advice or assistance is needed, consult with a doctor. This book is considered a guide and should not be used in any way detrimental to your health. Consult with a physician before starting this nutritional plan to make sure it's right for you.

## ACKNOWLEDGEMENTS

This book is dedicated to my friends and family that have had mild or serious illnesses so that you may find a solution and make the necessary changes in your life.

# 42 Juicing Solutions for the Common Fever:

## Reduce and Lower Fevers without Recurring to Pills or Medicine

By

Joe Correa CSN

# CONTENTS

Copyright

Acknowledgements

About The Author

Introduction

Commitment

42 Juicing Solutions for the Common Fever: Reduce and Lower Fevers without Recurring to Pills or Medicine

Additional Titles from This Author

## ABOUT THE AUTHOR

After years of Research, I honestly believe in the positive effects that proper nutrition can have over the body and mind. My knowledge and experience has helped me live healthier throughout the years and which I have shared with family and friends. The more you know about eating and drinking healthier, the sooner you will want to change your life and eating habits.

Nutrition is a key part in the process of being healthy and living longer so get started today. The first step is the most important and the most significant.

## INTRODUCTION

42 Juicing Solutions for the Common Fever: Reduce and Lower Fevers without Recurring to Pills or Medicine

By Joe Correa CSN

Although it sounds scary, having a fever is actually a sign that your body is fighting some out of the ordinary condition. A fever can be recognized by an increase in body temperature which usually occurs after an illness or some other health issue. This uncomfortable condition usually goes away on its own after just a couple of days and shouldn't be a reason for concern unless the temperature reaches 103F.

Some typical symptoms of fever include:

- Abnormal sweating which is not caused by some physical activity or high external temperature
- Sudden chills and shivering without any good reason
- A severe and sudden headache that lasts for hours
- Constant muscle aches throughout the entire body
- Complete loss of appetite
- Mild dehydration
- An overall and general weakness of the body

As I said earlier, these common fever symptoms are harmless most of the time and shouldn't be a reason for concern. There are, however, some cases when you should visit a doctor. These include severe headaches which can't be cured with your standard painkillers, skin rashes, mental confusion, constant vomiting, or difficulty breathing.

There are plenty of over-the-counter medications which can help reduce the symptoms of a fever but in some cases, it's much better to leave your body to heal on its own. Getting plenty of rest and eating the rights foods can help your body boost its immune system and speed up the healing process. This way, you will give your body the opportunity to defend itself in the most natural way possible without eliminating natural mechanisms of defense.

This book was created to help you reduce those unpleasant symptoms and heal your body faster than ever before. It is a beautiful collection of 42 juice recipes that are based on natural and healthy ingredients which are loaded with vitamins and minerals. These juices have the ability to boost up your immune system and make your body work on its own healing mechanisms. Furthermore, including these juices into your daily meal plan will improve your overall health and prevent similar problems from occurring in the future. Take a couple of minutes in the morning or in the afternoon and prepare yourself a juice that will do wonders for your body and health. Enjoy!

# 42 JUICING SOLUTIONS FOR THE COMMON FEVER

1. **Sweet Kale Avocado Juice**

**Ingredients:**

1 cup fresh kale, torn

1 artichoke heart, chopped

1 cup avocado, cubed

1 large cucumber, sliced

1 cup green cabbage, torn

1 tbsp liquid honey

**Preparation:**

Using a sharp knife, trim off the outer leaves of the artichoke. Wash it and cut into small pieces. Set aside.

Peel the avocado and cut in half. Remove the pit and cut into cubes. Reserve the rest of the avocado for some other juice. Set aside.

Wash the cucumber and cut into thick slices. Set aside.

Wash the basil and cabbage thoroughly and torn with hands. Set aside.

Now, process artichoke, avocado, cucumber, basil, and cabbage in a juicer. Transfer to serving glasses and stir in the liquid honey.

Refrigerate for 30 minutes before serving.

**Nutrition information per serving:** Kcal: 379, Protein: 14.2g, Carbs: 73.6g, Fats: 22.8g

## 2. Peach Kiwi Juice

**Ingredients:**

5 medium-sized apricots, sliced

1 large peach, sliced

1 large kiwi, peeled

A bunch of fresh spinach, chopped

1 tbsp fresh mint, chopped

¼ cup of water

**Preparation:**

Wash the peach and cut in half. Remove the pit and cut into small pieces. Set aside.

Peel the kiwi and cut lengthwise in half. Set aside.

Wash the apricots and cut in half. Remove the pits and cut into chunks. Set aside.

Wash the spinach and mint under cold running water. Drain and roughly chop it. Set aside.

Now, combine peach, kiwi, apricots, spinach, and mint in a juicer and process until juiced.

Transfer to serving glasses and refrigerate before serving.

**Nutrition information per serving:** Kcal: 211, Protein: 2.8g, Carbs: 58.8g, Fats: 2.8g

## 3. Blueberry Strawberry Juice

**Ingredients:**

1 cup blueberries

1 cup strawberries

1 cup cranberries

1 cup raspberries

1 cup blackberries

1 small Granny Smith's apple

¼ cup water

1 tsp pure coconut sugar

2 oz of water

**Preparation:**

Combine all berries in a colander and rinse under cold running water. Cut the strawberries in half and set aside.

Soak the berries in water for 10 minutes. Drain and set aside.

Wash the apple and remove the core. Cut into bite-sized pieces and set aside.

Now, process all berries and apple in a juicer. Transfer to serving glasses and stir in the coconut sugar and water.

Add some ice and serve immediately.

**Nutrition information per serving:** Kcal: 210, Protein: 5.7g, Carbs: 82g, Fats: 2.4g

## 4. Cucumber Lemon Juice

**Ingredients:**

1 whole cucumber, sliced

1 large lemon, peeled

5 large plums, pitted and halved

1 cup purple cabbage, torn

1 cup beets, trimmed

2 oz water

**Preparation:**

Wash the cucumber and cut into thick slices. Set aside.

Peel the lemon and cut lengthwise in half. Set aside.

Wash the plums and cut in half. Remove the pits and cut into quarters. Set aside.

Wash the cabbage thoroughly under cold running water. Drain and torn with hands.

Wash the beets and trim off the green parts. Cut into bite-sized pieces and set aside.

Now, process cucumber, lemon, plums, cabbage, and beets in a juicer.

Transfer to serving glasses and add some ice before serving.

Enjoy!

**Nutrition information per serving:** Kcal: 243, Protein: 8.3g, Carbs: 73.6g, Fats: 1.7g

## 5. Lettuce Cauliflower Juice

**Ingredients:**

1 cup Iceberg lettuce, chopped

1 cup cauliflower, chopped

1 cup turnip greens, chopped

1 cup kale, chopped

1 large cucumber, sliced

**Preparation:**

Combine Iceberg lettuce, turnip greens, and kale in a colander and wash under cold running water. Drain and roughly chop it. Set aside.

Trim off the outer leaves of cauliflower. Wash it and cut into small pieces. Fill the measuring cup and reserve the rest for some other juice. Set aside.

Wash the cucumber and cut into thick slices. Set aside.

Now, combine Iceberg lettuce, turnip greens, kale, cauliflower, and cucumber in a juicer and process until juiced.

Transfer to serving glasses and add some ice before serving.

Enjoy!

**Nutrition information per serving:** Kcal: 96, Protein: 8.3g, Carbs: 27.6g, Fats: 1.6g

## 6. Apple Kale Juice

**Ingredients:**

1 large Honeycrisp apple, cored

1 cup fresh kale, chopped

1 medium-sized fennel bulb

1 cup of mustard greens, torn

1 large red bell pepper, seeded

1 tbsp liquid honey

**Preparation:**

Wash the apple and remove the core. Cut into bite-sized pieces and set aside.

Combine kale and mustard greens in a colander. Wash under cold running water and torn with hands. Set aside.

Wash the fennel bulb and trim off the wilted outer layers. Cut into small chunks and set aside.

Wash the bell pepper and cut in half. Remove the seeds and chop into small slices. Set aside.

Now, process fennel, apple, kale, mustard greens, and bell pepper in a juicer.

Transfer to serving glasses and stir in the honey. Refrigerate for 10 minutes before serving.

**Nutrition information per serving:** Kcal: 258, Protein: 9.5g, Carbs: 88.4g, Fats: 3.2g

## 7. Spicy Watermelon Juice

**Ingredients:**

2 cups watermelon, seeded

1/8 tsp Jalapeno pepper, ground

1 cup Romaine lettuce, chopped

1 large orange, peeled

1 cup fresh broccoli, chopped

**Preparation:**

Cut the watermelon lengthwise. For two cups, you will need about two large wedges. Peel and cut into chunks. Remove the seeds and set aside. Reserve the rest of the melon for some other juices.

Combine lettuce and broccoli in a colander and rinse under cold running water. Drain and chop into small pieces. Set aside.

Peel the orange and divide into wedges. Set aside.

Now, process watermelon, lettuce, broccoli, and orange in a juicer.

Transfer to serving glasses and stir in the jalapeno pepper for some extra spicy flavor. Refrigerate for 10 minutes before serving.

Enjoy!

**Nutrition information per serving:** Kcal: 185, Protein: 5g, Carbs: 52.8g, Fats: 1.3g

## 8. Swiss Chard Cucumber Juice

**Ingredients:**

2 cups Swiss chard, torn

1 large cucumber, sliced

1 cup fresh parsley, torn

1 medium-sized Zestar apple, cored

1 small orange, peeled

**Preparation:**

Combine Swiss chard and parsley in a colander and wash thoroughly under cold running water. Drain and torn with hands. Set aside.

Wash the cucumber and cut into thick slices. Set aside.

Wash the apple and remove the core. Cut into bite-sized pieces and set aside.

Peel the orange and divide into wedges. Set aside.

Now, combine Swiss chard, parsley, cucumber, apple, and orange in a juicer and process until juiced. Transfer to serving glasses and add some ice before serving.

Enjoy!

**Nutrition information per serving:** Kcal: 161, Protein: 6.3g, Carbs: 46.3g, Fats: 1.2g

## 9. Raspberry Carrot Juice

**Ingredients:**

1 large grapefruit, peeled

1 cup raspberries

1 large carrot, sliced

1 medium-sized Granny Smith's apple, cored

1 small ginger root slice, 1-inch

1 oz water

**Preparation:**

Place the raspberries in a colander and rinse under cold running water. Drain and set aside.

Wash the carrot and cut into thick slices. Set aside.

Peel the grapefruit and divide into wedges. Set aside.

Wash the apple and remove the core. Cut into bite-sized pieces. Set aside.

Peel the ginger root and set aside.

Now, process raspberries, carrot, grapefruit, apple, and ginger in a juicer.

Transfer to serving glasses and stir in the water. Add few

ice cubes or refrigerate before serving.

Enjoy!

**Nutrition information per serving:** Kcal: 239, Protein: 4.9g, Carbs: 76.2g, Fats: 1.7g

## 10. Pomegranate Kale Juice

**Ingredients:**

1 cup pomegranate seeds

1 cup fresh kale, torn

1 large lemon, peeled

1 cup watercress, torn

1 cup Swiss chard, torn

1 bunch fresh spinach, torn

1 oz water

1 tsp agave nectar

**Preparation:**

Combine kale, watercress, Swiss chard, and spinach in a colander. Rinse thoroughly under cold running water. Drain and torn with hands. Set aside.

Cut the top of the pomegranate fruit using a sharp knife. Slice down to each of the white membranes inside of the fruit. Pop the seeds into a bowl and set aside.

Peel the lemon and cut lengthwise in half. Set aside.

Now, process, pomegranate seeds, lemon, kale, watercress, Swiss chard, and spinach in a juicer.

Transfer to serving glasses and add few ice cubes before serving.

Enjoy!

**Nutrition information per serving:** Kcal: 372, Protein: 12.1g, Carbs: 68.6g, Fats: 22.8g

## 11.     Apple Cucumber Juice

**Ingredients:**

2 small green apples, cored

1 large cucumber, sliced

1 medium-sized carrot, sliced

1 large beet, trimmed

1 small ginger knob, 1 inch

**Preparation:**

Wash the apples and remove the core. Cut into bite-sized pieces and set aside.

Wash the cucumber and carrot. Cut into thick slices and set aside.

Wash the beet and trim off the green parts. Cut into small pieces and set aside.

Peel the ginger root knob and set aside.

Now, combine apple, cucumber, carrot, beet, and ginger in a juicer and process until juiced.

Transfer to serving glasses and add some ice cubes and serve immediately.

Enjoy!

**Nutrition information per serving:** Kcal: 166, Protein: 4.7g, Carbs: 48.4g, Fats: 0.9g

## 12. Watermelon Cranberries Juice

**Ingredients:**

1 cup watermelon, chopped

1 cup cranberries

1 large banana, sliced

1 whole kiwi, peeled

5 large strawberries, chopped

**Preparation:**

Cut the watermelon lengthwise. For one cup, you will need a large slice. Peel and cut into chunks. Remove the seeds and set aside. Reserve the rest for some other juices.

Rinse the cranberries thoroughly and slightly drain. Set aside.

Peel the banana and cut into thin slices. Set aside.

Peel the kiwi and cut lengthwise in half. Set aside.

Wash the strawberries and cut into bite-sized pieces. Set aside.

Now, combine watermelon, cranberries, banana, kiwi, and strawberries in a juicer and process until juiced.

Transfer to a serving glass and add some ice before serving.

Enjoy!

**Nutritional information per serving**: Kcal: 236, Protein: 4.3g, Carbs: 72.9g, Fats: 1.4g

## 13. Mandarin Orange Juice

**Ingredients:**

2 mandarin oranges, wedged

1 cup blueberries

1 cup cherries, pitted

1 cup green grapes

¼ tsp cinnamon, ground

**Preparation:**

Peel the mandarin oranges and divide into wedges. Set aside.

Combine blueberries and grapes in a colander and wash under cold running water. Slightly drain and set aside.

Wash the cherries and cut each in half. Remove the pits and set aside.

Now, combine oranges, blueberries, cherries, and grapes in a juicer and process until juiced.

Transfer to a serving glass and stir in the cinnamon.

Add some ice and serve immediately.

**Nutritional information per serving**: Kcal: 249, Protein: 4.2g, Carbs: 73.2g, Fats: 1.2g

## 14. Pomegranate Pear Juice

**Ingredients:**

1 cup pomegranate seeds

1 small pear, chopped

1 medium-sized orange, peeled

1 small zucchini, chopped

1 cup fresh mint, torn

1 tbsp liquid honey

**Preparation:**

Cut the top of the pomegranate fruit using a sharp paring knife. Slice down to each of the white membranes inside of the fruit. Pop the seeds into a measuring cup and set aside.

Wash the pear and cut in half. Remove the core and cut into bite-sized pieces. Set aside.

Peel the orange and divide into wedges. Cut each wedge in half and set aside.

Peel the zucchini and cut into small chunks. Set aside.

Rinse the mint under cold running water using a colander. Slightly drain and torn with hands. Set aside.

Now, combine pomegranate seeds, pear, orange, zucchini, and mint in a juicer and process until juiced. Transfer to a serving glass and stir in the honey.

Add some crushed ice and serve immediately.

**Nutritional information per serving**: Kcal: 259, Protein: 5.6g, Carbs: 61.6g, Fats: 2.1g

## 15. Cranberry Watercress Juice

**Ingredients:**

2 large pears, chopped

1 cup cranberries

1 cup watercress, torn

½ cup fresh spinach, torn

1 small ginger knob, peeled

**Preparation:**

Place the cranberries in a colander and rinse thoroughly. Slightly drain and set aside.

Wash watercress and spinach thoroughly under cold running water. Drain and torn with hands. Set aside.

Wash the pears and cut in half. Remove the core and cut into bite-sized pieces. Set aside.

Peel the ginger and set aside.

Now, combine cranberries, watercress, pears, spinach, and ginger in a juicer and process until well juiced. Transfer to a serving glass and stir in some water if you like. However, it is optional.

Refrigerate for 10 minutes before serving.

Enjoy!

**Nutritional information per serving**: Kcal: 249, Protein: 3.8g, Carbs: 86.1g, Fats: 0.9g

## 16. Avocado Mango Juice

**Ingredients:**

1 cup avocado, chunked

1 cup mango, chopped

1 small zucchini, chopped

1 whole lime, peeled

1 oz coconut water

1 tsp fresh mint, finely chopped

**Preparation:**

Peel the avocado and cut in half. Remove the pit and cut into chunks. Set aside.

Wash and peel the mango. Chop into bite-sized pieces and set aside.

Peel the zucchini and cut lengthwise in half. Scrape out the seeds and wash it. Cut into small pieces and set aside.

Peel the lime and cut lengthwise in half. Set aside.

Now, combine avocado, mango, zucchini, lime, and mint in a juicer and process until juiced. Transfer to a serving glass and stir in the coconut water. Add some crushed ice and serve immediately.

**Nutritional information per serving**: Kcal: 309, Protein: 5.8g, Carbs: 44.5g, Fats: 22.4g

## 17.   Grape Kiwi Juice

**Ingredients:**

1 cup green grapes

1 whole kiwi, peeled

1 cup watermelon, cubed

1 medium-sized pear, chopped

1 tsp agave nectar

**Preparation:**

Wash the grapes and set aside.

Peel the kiwi and cut lengthwise in half. Set aside.

Cut the watermelon lengthwise. Cut one large wedge and peel it. Cut into chunks and fill the measuring cup. Remove the seeds and set aside. Reserve the rest of the melon for some other juices.

Wash the pear and remove the core. Cut into bite-sized pieces and set aside.

Now, combine grapes, kiwi, watermelon, and pear in a juicer and process until well juiced.

Transfer to a serving glass and stir in the agave nectar. Add some crushed ice before serving.

Enjoy!

**Nutritional information per serving**: Kcal: 236, Protein: 3g, Carbs: 70.5g, Fats: 1.2g

## 18. Avocado Pomegranate Juice

**Ingredients:**

1 cup strawberries, chopped

1 cup avocado, cubed

1 pomegranate seeds

1 cup cucumber, sliced

1 medium-sized orange, wedged

**Preparation:**

Peel the avocado and cut in half. Remove the pit and cut into cubes. Fill the measuring cup and reserve the rest for later.

Cut the top of the pomegranate fruit using a sharp paring knife. Slice down to each of the white membranes inside of the fruit. Pop the seeds into a measuring cup and set aside.

Wash the strawberries and cut into small pieces. Set aside.

Wash the cucumber and cut into thin slices. Fill the measuring cup and reserve the rest for later.

Peel the orange and divide into wedges. Chop each wedge in half and set aside.

Now, combine avocado, pomegranate, strawberries, cucumber, and orange in a juicer. Process until well juiced.

Transfer to a serving glass and add some crushed ice before serving.

**Nutritional information per serving**: Kcal: 335, Protein: 6.6g, Carbs: 53.2g, Fats: 23.5g

## 19. Cherry Lime Juice

**Ingredients:**

1 cup fresh cherries, pitted

1 whole lime, peeled

1 cup avocado, cubed

1 medium-sized orange, wedged

1 tbsp honey, raw

**Preparation:**

Wash the cherries and cut each in half. Remove the pits and set aside.

Peel the lime and cut lengthwise in half. Set aside.

Peel the avocado and cut in half. Remove the pit and cut into small cubes. Fill the measuring cup and reserve the rest for later.

Peel the orange and divide into wedges. Cut each wedge in half and set aside.

Now, combine cherries, lime, avocado, and orange in a juicer and process until well juiced. Transfer to a serving glass and stir in the honey.

Add some crushed ice and serve.

**Nutritional information per serving**: Kcal: 408, Protein: 6g, Carbs: 74.5g, Fats: 22.5g

## 20. Broccoli Apple Juice

**Ingredients:**

1 cup cauliflower, chopped

1 cup broccoli, chopped

1 small Granny Smith's apple, cored

1 cup fresh kale, torn

¼ tsp ginger, ground

**Preparation:**

Wash the broccoli thoroughly and chop into small pieces. Set aside.

Wash the apple and cut lengthwise in half. Remove the core and cut into bite-sized pieces. Set aside.

Wash the cauliflower and trim off the outer leaves. Cut into small pieces and set aside.

Rinse the kale under cold running water and slightly drain. Torn with hands and set aside.

Now, combine broccoli, apple, cauliflower, and kale in a juicer and process until well juiced. Transfer to a serving glass and stir in the ground ginger.

Refrigerate for 10-15 minutes before serving.

**Nutritional information per serving**: Kcal: 131, Protein: 8.1g, Carbs: 36.8g, Fats: 1.5g

## 21. Apple Mint Juice

**Ingredients:**

1 medium-sized Granny Smith's apple, cored

1 cup fresh mint, torn

2 cups Brussels sprouts, halved

1 cup fresh kale, torn

1 whole lime, peeled

1 oz water

**Preparation:**

Wash the apple and cut in half. Remove the core and cut into bite-sized pieces. Set aside.

Combine mint and kale in a large colander and rinse under cold running water. Slightly drain and torn with hands. Set aside.

Wash the Brussels sprouts and trim off the outer leaves. Cut in half and fill the measuring cup. Reserve the rest for later.

Peel the lime and cut lengthwise in half. Set aside.

Now, combine apple, mint, Brussels sprouts, kale, and lime in a juicer and process until juiced. Transfer to a serving glass and stir in the water.

Refrigerate for 5 minutes before serving.

Enjoy!

**Nutritional information per serving**: Kcal: 171, Protein: 10.6g, Carbs: 51.7g, Fats: 1.7g

## 22. Plum Lemon Juice

**Ingredients:**

2 medium-sized peaches, pitted

2 whole plums, pitted

1 whole lemon, peeled

1 cup watermelon

¼ tsp ginger, ground

**Preparation:**

Wash the plums and cut lengthwise in half. Remove the pits and set aside.

Peel the lemons and cut lengthwise in half. Set aside.

Wash the peaches and cut in half. Remove the pits and cut into bite-sized pieces. Set aside.

Cut the watermelon lengthwise. For one cup, you will need a large slice. Peel and cut into chunks. Remove the seeds and set aside. Reserve the rest for some other juices.

Now, combine plums, lemon, peaches, and watermelon in a juicer and process until juiced. Transfer to a serving glass and stir in the ginger. For some extra taste, add some freshly grated lemon zest. However, it's optional.

Refrigerate for 10 minutes before serving.

**Nutritional information per serving**: Kcal: 205, Protein: 5.2g, Carbs: 60.6g, Fats: 1.5g

## 23. Lemon Peach Juice

**Ingredients:**

1 whole lemon, peeled

1 large peach, pitted

1 large Zestar apple, cored

1 medium-sized carrot, chopped

¼ tsp cinnamon, ground

2 oz water

**Preparation:**

Peel the lemon and cut lengthwise in half. Set aside.

Wash the peach and cut in half. Remove the pit and cut into bite-sized pieces. Set aside.

Wash the apple and cut lengthwise in half. Remove the core and cut into bite-sized pieces. Set aside.

Wash and peel the carrot. Cut into small chunks and set aside.

Now, combine lemon, peach, apple, and carrot in a juicer. Process until nicely juiced. Transfer to a serving glass and stir in the water and cinnamon.

Add some ice or refrigerate for 5 minutes before serving.

Enjoy!

**Nutritional information per serving**: Kcal: 165, Protein: 3.6g, Carbs: 50.7g, Fats: 1.1g

## 24. Mango Banana Juice

**Ingredients:**

1 cup mango, chunked

1 medium-sized banana, chopped

1 large guava, chopped

1 large orange, wedged

1 oz coconut water

**Preparation:**

Wash and peel the mango and guava. Cut into small chunks and set aside.

Peel the banana and cut into small chunks. Set aside.

Peel the orange and divide into wedges. Set aside.

Now, combine mango, banana, guava, and orange in a juicer and process until well juiced. Transfer to a serving glass and stir in the water.

Add some ice and serve immediately.

Enjoy!

**Nutritional information per serving**: Kcal: 275, Protein: 5.7g, Carbs: 81.1g, Fats: 1.8g

## 25. Broccoli Beet Greens Juice

**Ingredients:**

1 cup broccoli, chopped

1 cup beet greens, torn

1 cup fresh basil, torn

1 large lemon, peeled

1 medium-sized Honeycrisp apple, cored

1 cup cauliflower, chopped

**Preparation:**

Wash the broccoli and chop into small pieces. Set aside.

Combine beet greens and basil in a large colander. Rinse under cold running water and drain. Torn with hands and set aside.

Peel the lemon and cut lengthwise in half. Set aside.

Wash the apple and cut lengthwise in half. Remove the core and cut into bite-sized pieces. Set aside.

Trim off the outer leaves of a cauliflower. Wash it and fill and cut into small pieces. Fill the measuring cup and reserve the rest in the refrigerator.

Now, combine broccoli, beet greens, basil, lemon, apple, and cauliflower in a juicer. Process until well juiced and transfer to a serving glass.

Add few ice cubes and serve immediately.

**Nutritional information per serving**: Kcal: 137, Protein: 7.3g, Carbs: 42.1g, Fats: 1.3g

## 26. Carrot Orange Juice

**Ingredients:**

2 large carrots, peeled and chopped

1 large orange, wedged

1 cup raspberries

¼ tsp ginger, ground

1 tbsp liquid honey

**Preparation:**

Wash the carrots and peel them. Cut into small chunks and set aside.

Peel the orange and divide into wedges. Set aside.

Using a colander, rinse the raspberries under cold running water and drain. Set aside.

Now, combine raspberries, carrots, and orange in a juicer and process until well juiced. Transfer to a serving glass and stir in the ginger and honey.

Refrigerate for 10 minutes before serving.

**Nutritional information per serving**: Kcal: 204, Protein: 4.5g, Carbs: 67.1g, Fats: 1.3g

## 27. Lemon Celery Juice

**Ingredients:**

1 large lemon, peeled

3 large celery stalks, chopped

1 large Granny Smith's apple, cored

1 large cucumber

2 oz coconut water

**Preparation:**

Peel the lemon and cut lengthwise in half. Set aside.

Wash the celery stalks and cut into small pieces. Set aside.

Wash the apple and cut lengthwise in half. Remove the core and cut into small chunks. Set aside.

Peel the cucumber and cut into small chunks. Set aside.

Now, combine lemon, celery, apple, and cucumber in a juicer and process until well juiced. Transfer to serving glasses and stir in the coconut water.

Add few ice cubes and serve immediately.

Enjoy!

**Nutritional information per serving**: Kcal: 175, Protein: 5.1g, Carbs: 50.2g, Fats: 1.3g

## 28. Spinach Lettuce Juice

**Ingredients:**

1 cup fresh spinach, torn

1 cup Iceberg lettuce, shredded

1 cup fresh coriander, chopped

1 whole cucumber, sliced

¼ tsp salt

**Preparation:**

Combine spinach, coriander, and lettuce in a large colander. Wash thoroughly under cold running water and slightly drain. Roughly chop all and set aside.

Wash the cucumber and cut into thin slices. Set aside.

Now, combine spinach, lettuce, coriander, and cucumber in a juicer and process until well juiced.

Transfer to a serving glass and stir in the salt. Optionally, add some ground pepper or even cayenne pepper for some spicy taste.

Serve immediately.

**Nutrition information per serving:** Kcal: 85, Protein: 10.3g, Carbs: 23.9g, Fats: 1.8g

## 29.   Cabbage Beet Juice

**Ingredients:**

1 cup purple cabbage, torn

1 whole beet, chopped

1 cup broccoli, chopped

1 cup Swiss chard, torn

1 cup cucumber, sliced

¼ tsp turmeric, ground

**Preparation:**

Combine purple cabbage and Swiss chard in a large colander. Wash thoroughly under cold running water and slightly drain. Torn with hands and set aside.

Wash the beets and trim off the green parts. Cut into bite-sized pieces and set aside.

Wash the broccoli and trim off the outer layers. Chop it into small pieces and set aside.

Wash the cucumber and cut into thin slices. Fill the measuring cup and reserve the rest for later. Set aside.

Now, combine purple cabbage, beet, broccoli, Swiss chard, and cucumber in a juicer and process until juiced.

Transfer to a serving glass and stir in the turmeric. Refrigerate for 15 minutes and serve.

Enjoy!

**Nutrition information per serving:** Kcal: 79, Protein: 6.2g, Carbs: 23.7g, Fats: 0.8g

## 30. Lime Cucumber Juice

**Ingredients:**

1 whole lime, peeled

1 cup cucumber, sliced

2 medium-sized carrots, sliced

1 medium-sized orange, wedged

1 tbsp honey

**Preparation:**

Peel the lime and cut lengthwise in half. Set aside.

Wash the cucumber and cut into thin slices. Fill the measuring cup and reserve the rest for later.

Wash and peel the carrots. Cut into thin slices and set aside.

Peel the orange and divide into wedges. Cut each wedge in half and set aside.

Now, combine lime, cucumber, carrots, and orange in a juicer and process until juiced. Transfer to a serving glass and stir in the honey.

Add some ice before serving.

Enjoy!

**Nutrition information per serving:** Kcal: 163, Protein: 2.9g, Carbs: 32.6g, Fats: 0.6g

## 31. Red Orange Lemon Juice

**Ingredients:**

1 large red orange, peeled

1 whole lemon, peeled

1 medium-sized artichoke, chopped

1 whole lime, peeled

1 tbsp liquid honey

1 oz water

**Preparation:**

Peel the orange and divide into wedges. Cut each wedge in half and set aside.

Peel the lemon and lime. Cut each fruit lengthwise in half and set aside.

Trim off the outer layers of the artichoke using a sharp paring knife. Cut into bite-sized pieces and set aside.

Now, combine orange, lemon, artichoke, and lime in a juicer. Process until well juiced. Transfer to a serving glass and stir in the honey and water.

Refrigerate for 15 minutes before serving.

**Nutrition information per serving:** Kcal: 149, Protein: 5.9g, Carbs: 33.8g, Fats: 0.5g

## 32. Kale Lime Juice

**Ingredients:**

1 cup cauliflower, chopped

1 cup fresh kale, chopped

1 whole lime, peeled

1 cup cucumber, sliced

1 tsp agave nectar

**Preparation:**

Wash the kale thoroughly under cold running water and slightly drain. Chop into small pieces and set aside.

Peel the lime and cut lengthwise in half. Set aside.

Trim off the outer layer of the cauliflower. Cut into bite-sized pieces and wash it. Fill the measuring cup and sprinkle with some salt. Set aside.

Wash the cucumber and cut into thin slices. Fill the measuring cup and reserve the rest for some other juice. Set aside.

Now, combine kale, lime, cauliflower, and cucumber in a juicer. Process until well juiced. Transfer to a serving glass and stir in the agave nectar.

Refrigerate before serving.

Enjoy!

**Nutrition information per serving:** Kcal: 107, Protein: 11.4g, Carbs: 30.4g, Fats: 1.8g

## 33. Kiwi Peach Juice

**Ingredients:**

1 small apple, cored

1 whole kiwi, peeled

1 small peach, pitted

½ cup fresh spinach, torn

**Preparation:**

Peel the kiwi and cut lengthwise in half. Set aside.

Wash the peach and cut in half. Remove the pit and cut into bite-sized pieces. Set aside.

Wash the apple and cut in half. Remove the core and cut into bite-sized pieces. Set aside.

Rinse the spinach under cold running water and slightly drain. Torn with hands and set aside.

Now, combine kiwi, peach, apple, and spinach in a juicer and process until juiced. Transfer to a serving glass and add some ice.

Serve immediately.

**Nutrition information per serving:** Kcal: 165, Protein: 6.9g, Carbs: 47.6g, Fats: 1.5g

## 34. Cranberry Raspberry Juice

**Ingredients:**

1 cup of raspberries

1 cup of fresh mint, torn

1 cup of cranberries

1 whole lemon, peeled

1 medium-sized Zestar apple, cored

¼ tsp cinnamon, ground

**Preparation:**

Combine raspberries and cranberries in a large colander. Rinse thoroughly under cold running water and slightly drain. Set aside.

Rinse the mint and torn with hands. Set aside.

Peel the lemon and cut lengthwise in half. Set aside.

Wash the apple and cut in half. Remove the core and cut into bite-sized pieces.

Now, combine raspberries, mint, cranberries, lemon, and apple in a juicer and process until juiced. Transfer to a serving glass and stir in the cinnamon. Add some ice before serving.

Enjoy!

**Nutrition information per serving:** Kcal: 143, Protein: 3.8g, Carbs: 53.5g, Fats: 1.5g

## 35. Tropical Orange Juice

**Ingredients:**

1 medium-sized orange, peeled

1 large carrot, sliced

1 whole guava, peeled

1 whole lemon, peeled

1 tbsp liquid honey

**Preparation:**

Peel the orange and divide into wedges. Cut each wedge in half and set aside.

Wash and peel the carrot. Cut into thin slices and set aside.

Peel the guava with a sharp paring knife. Cut into small chunks and set aside.

Peel the lemon and cut lengthwise in half. Set aside.

Now, combine orange, carrot, guava, and lemon in a juicer and process until juiced. Transfer to a serving glass and stir in the honey.

Add some ice and serve immediately.

**Nutrition information per serving:** Kcal: 168, Protein: 3.9g, Carbs: 35.6g, Fats: 1.1g

## 36. Mango Pear Juice

**Ingredients:**

1 medium-sized pear, chopped

1 cup pomegranate seeds

1 cup mango, chunked

1 cup Iceberg lettuce, shredded

1 tbsp liquid honey

1 oz water

**Preparation:**

Wash the pear and cut into small pieces. Set aside.

Cut the top of the pomegranate fruit using a sharp paring knife. Slice down to each of the white membranes inside of the fruit. Pop the seeds into a measuring cup and set aside.

Peel the mango and cut into small chunks. Fill the measuring cup and reserve the rest in the refrigerator. Set aside.

Wash the lettuce thoroughly under cold running water and shred it. Fill the measuring cup and reserve the rest for later.

Now, combine pear, pomegranate, mango, and lettuce in a juicer and process until well juiced. Transfer to a serving glass and stir in the honey and water. Add some ice and serve immediately.

**Nutrition information per serving:** Kcal: 230, Protein: 4.1g, Carbs: 69.6g, Fats: 2.1g

## 37. Cherry Ginger Juice

**Ingredients:**

1 cup cherries, pitted

1 small ginger slice, peeled

1 cup apricots, pitted

1 oz of coconut water

**Preparation:**

Wash the cherries and remove the stems, if any. Cut each in half and remove the pits. Fill the measuring cup and set aside.

Peel the ginger slice and set aside.

Wash the apricots and cut in half. Remove the pits and cut into small pieces. Fill the measuring cup and set aside.

Now, combine cherries, ginger, and apricots in a juicer and process until well juiced. Transfer to a serving glass and stir in the coconut water. For a sweeter taste, add some honey. However, it's optional.

Refrigerate for 15 minutes before serving.

Enjoy!

**Nutrition information per serving:** Kcal: 149, Protein: 3.8g, Carbs: 40.8g, Fats: 0.9g

## 38.     Plum Apple Juice

**Ingredients:**

2 whole plums, chopped

1 medium-sized Granny Smith's apple, cored

1 cup avocado, cubed

1 whole lemon, peeled

¼ tsp cinnamon, ground

1 tbsp coconut water

**Preparation:**

Wash the plums and cut lengthwise in half. Remove the pits and cut into bite-sized pieces. Set aside.

Wash the apple and cut in half. Remove the pit and cut into small pieces. Set aside.

Peel the avocado and cut in half. Remove the pit and cut into small cubes. Fill the measuring cup and reserve the rest for later.

Peel the lemon and cut into half. Set aside.

Now, combine avocado, plums, apple, and lemon in a juicer and process until juiced. Transfer to a serving glass and stir in the cinnamon and coconut water.

Refrigerate for 10 minutes before serving.

Enjoy!

**Nutrition information per serving:** Kcal: 341, Protein: 5.3g, Carbs: 56.1g, Fats: 22.8g

## 39. Grape Apple Juice

**Ingredients:**

1 cup black grapes

1 small Golden Delicious apple, cored

1 cup cranberries

¼ tsp cinnamon, ground

**Preparation:**

Wash the grapes and fill the measuring cup. Reserve the rest for later.

Wash the apple and cut in half. Remove the core and cut into bite-sized pieces. Set aside.

Rinse the cranberries using a colander. Slightly drain and set aside.

Now, combine grapes, apple, and cranberries in a juicer and process until juiced. Transfer to a serving glass and stir in the cinnamon.

Add some ice before serving and enjoy!

**Nutritional information per serving:** Kcal: 190, Protein: 2.1g, Carbs: 56.7g, Fats: 1.1g

## 40. Pear Blueberry Juice

**Ingredients:**

1 medium-sized pear, chopped

1 cup blueberries

1 whole lemon, peeled

½ cup strawberries, sliced

1 small ginger knob, peeled

1 oz water

**Preparation:**

Wash the pear and cut in half. Remove the core and cut into small pieces. Set aside.

Rinse the blueberries and fill the measuring cup. Set aside.

Peel the lemon and cut in half. Set aside.

Wash the strawberries and remove the stems. Cut into small pieces and fill the measuring cup. Set aside.

Peel the ginger knob and set aside.

Now, combine pear, blueberries, lemon, strawberries, and ginger in a juicer and process until juiced. Transfer to a serving glass and stir in the water.

Serve cold.

**Nutritional information per serving:** Kcal: 143, Protein: 2.4g, Carbs: 52.7g, Fats: 0.8g

## 41. Banana Cinnamon Juice

**Ingredients:**

1 large banana, peeled

¼ tsp cinnamon, ground

1 medium-sized watermelon wedge

1 whole lime, peeled

1 small Granny Smith's apple, cored

**Preparation:**

Peel the banana and chop into small chunks. Set aside.

Cut one large watermelon wedge and peel it. Remove the seeds and cut into bite-sized pieces. Wrap the rest of the melon in a plastic foil and refrigerate.

Peel the lime and cut lengthwise in half. Set aside.

Wash the apple and cut in half. Remove the core and cut into bite-sized pieces. Set aside.

Now, combine banana melon, lime, and apple in a juicer and process until juiced. Transfer to a serving glass and stir in the cinnamon.

Refrigerate for 15 minutes before serving.

**Nutritional information per serving:** Kcal: 226, Protein: 4.6g, Carbs: 29.4g, Fats: 1.2g

## 42. Green Kiwi Spinach Juice

**Ingredients:**

1 whole kiwi, peeled

1 cup fresh spinach, chopped

1 cup mango, chunked

1 small ginger knob, peeled

2 tbsp coconut water

**Preparation:**

Peel the kiwi and cut lengthwise in half. Set aside.

Wash the spinach thoroughly under cold running water. Slightly drain and chop it into small pieces. Set aside.

Peel the mango and cut into small chunks. Fill the measuring cup and reserve the rest in the refrigerator.

Peel the ginger knob and set aside.

Now, combine kiwi, spinach, mango, and ginger in a juicer and process until juiced. Transfer to a serving glass and stir in the coconut water. Refrigerate for 10 minutes before serving.

Enjoy!

**Nutritional information per serving:** Kcal: 190, Protein: 9.1g, Carbs: 53.6g, Fats: 2.2g

## ADDITIONAL TITLES FROM THIS AUTHOR

70 Effective Meal Recipes to Prevent and Solve Being Overweight: Burn Fat Fast by Using Proper Dieting and Smart Nutrition

By Joe Correa CSN


48 Acne Solving Meal Recipes: The Fast and Natural Path to Fixing Your Acne Problems in Less Than 10 Days!

By Joe Correa CSN


41 Alzheimer's Preventing Meal Recipes: Reduce or Eliminate Your Alzheimer's Condition in 30 Days or Less!

By Joe Correa CSN


70 Effective Breast Cancer Meal Recipes: Prevent and Fight Breast Cancer with Smart Nutrition and Powerful Foods

By Joe Correa CSN

www.ingramcontent.com/pod-product-compliance
Lightning Source LLC
Chambersburg PA
CBHW060340080526
44584CB00013B/856